Questions and Answers: Countries

Liberia

A Question and Answer Book

by Muriel L. Dubois

Consultant:
Dr. Thomas O'Toole
Professor of Anthropology
St. Cloud State University
St. Cloud, Minnesota

Capstone
press

Mankato, Minnesota

Fact Finders is published by Capstone Press,
151 Good Counsel Drive, P.O. Box 669, Mankato, Minnesota 56002.
www.capstonepress.com

Library of Congress Cataloging-in-Publication Data
Dubois, Muriel L.
    Liberia: a question and answer book / by Muriel L. Dubois.
    p. cm.—(Fact finders. Questions and answers. Countries)
    Includes bibliographical references and index.
    ISBN 0-7368-3755-8 (hardcover)
    1. Liberia—Juvenile literature. I. Title. II. Series.
DT624.D83 2005
966.62—dc22   2004009811

Summary: Describes the geography, history, economy, and culture of Liberia in a
    question-and-answer format.

Editorial Credits
Donald Lemke, editor; Kia Adams, set designer; Kate Opseth, book designer; Nancy Steers,
    map illustrator; Wanda Winch, photo researcher; Scott Thoms, photo editor

Photo Credits
Beryl Goldberg, cover (background), 15, 16
Bishop Judith Craig Children's Village, Dwason, Liberia/Moses Banks, cover (foreground)
Corbis, 7; Paul Almasy, 23
Don Bosco Programs, Monrovia, Liberia/John T. Monibah, 20, 21
Getty Images Inc./Stephen Chernin, 9
Panos Pictures/Heldur Netocny, 1, 27; Jacob Silberberg, 11; Liba Taylor, 25
Peter Arnold Inc./Lineair Fotoarchief/Ron Gilling, 17, 18–19
Photo courtesy of Paul Baker, 29 (coins)
Photo courtesy of Richard Sutherland, 29 (bill)
Photri MicroStock, 4, 12–13
StockHaus Ltd., 29 (flag)

Table of Contents

Features

Where is Liberia?

Liberia is in western Africa. It is slightly larger than the U.S. state of Tennessee.

Liberia is mostly flat with some rolling hills. In the past, rain forests covered much of the land. Today, about 30 percent of the country has forests. Liberia lost many trees to logging, farming, and rubber **plantations**.

Liberia's coastline gets more rain than the dry inland areas. ▶

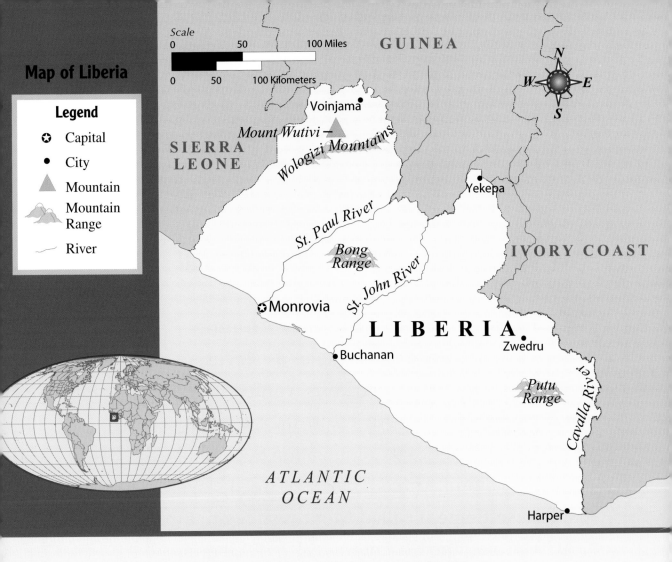

Map of Liberia

Legend

- ✪ Capital
- ● City
- ▲ Mountain
- Mountain Range
- — River

Mountains and rivers help form
Liberia's borders. Mount Wutivi in the
Wologizi Mountains is the country's tallest
point. This range stretches across part
of northern Liberia. The Cavalla River
divides southern Liberia from Ivory Coast.

When did Liberia become a country?

Liberia became an **independent** country on July 26, 1847. Before then, African **ethnic** groups ruled the area.

For hundreds of years, many Africans were taken to the United States as slaves. In the 1800s, some Americans wanted to send freed slaves back to Africa. In 1822, a group called the American Colonization Society (ACS) bought land in Africa. They sent freed slaves to start a **settlement** called Monrovia. Soon, the ACS formed the Commonwealth of Liberia.

Fact!

In 1824, Americo-Liberians named their settlement Monrovia after James Monroe, the U.S. president at the time.

In 1847, Joseph Jenkins Roberts became the first president of Liberia.

Settlers in Liberia faced many problems. People had little food. They fought with neighboring ethnic groups. The settlers also wanted to rule themselves.

In 1847, the ACS gave up control of the land. The next year, Liberian settlers elected their first leaders.

What type of government does Liberia have?

In July 1847, American settlers in Liberia formed Africa's first **republic**. This type of government is like the U.S. government. The settlers wrote a **constitution** and elected their own leaders.

Over time, African groups in Liberia became upset with the country's new leaders. In 1980, one of the groups took control of Liberia. Soon, other **rebel** groups tried to take power. In 1989, they started fighting against each other in a seven-year **civil war**.

Fact!

During the civil war (1989–1996), about 200,000 Liberians were killed and 1.5 million lost their homes.

Gyude Bryant became the leader of Liberia's temporary government in 2003.

Even after the war ended, the fighting continued. In 2003, Liberians finally signed a peace treaty. They created a temporary government that brings together leaders from all sides. It will help prepare the country for elections in 2005.

What kind of housing does Liberia have?

In Liberia's large cities, people live in small houses and apartments. Houses are often made of wood with tin roofs. Most apartments are made of brick. During the civil war, houses were destroyed. Many Liberians still live in camps for people without homes.

Where do people in Liberia live?

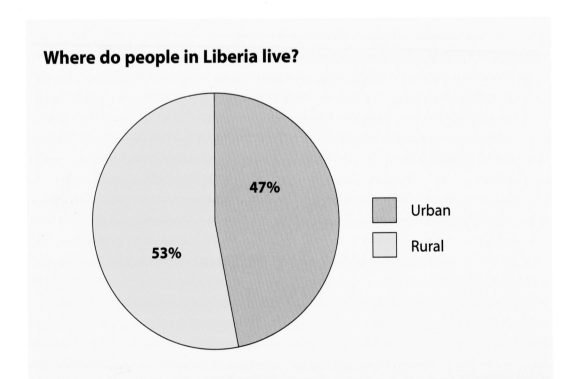

47%

53%

Urban

Rural

Most people in Monrovia live in crowded neighborhoods of small houses.

In areas outside cities, some families live in small, single-level houses. Others live in round houses made of mud. These houses have roofs made from palm leaves. They do not have electricity or running water. People get water from a village well.

What are Liberia's forms of transportation?

In cities, many people ride in taxis or crowded buses. Few people own cars. Most roads in Liberia are dirt. During the rainy season, vehicles get stuck in the mud. Liberians often have to walk to stores, work, and school.

Some Liberians fly in airplanes to neighboring countries. The main airport in Liberia is Roberts International Airport. It is located outside of Monrovia.

Fact!

Liberia does not have any working traffic lights. People often walk across the road with little or no warning.

Many Liberians have to walk from place to place.

Shipping goods in Liberia can be difficult. Many of Liberia's railroad lines were destroyed during the civil war. Today, many goods are moved by boat along the coast.

What are Liberia's major industries?

Rubber is one of Liberia's most important **exports**. Large companies collect a material called latex from the country's rubber trees. Latex is used to make rubber.

Today, many farmers grow just enough food to feed their families. They grow rice and sugarcane. They also grow coffee, cocoa, and tropical fruits. Some farmers raise pigs, sheep, and other animals.

What does Liberia import and export?	
Imports	*Exports*
chemicals	iron
fuels	rubber
machinery	timber

Rubber companies collect latex from rubber trees in Liberia.

Forestry and mining are other important industries in Liberia. Workers cut trees for lumber and firewood. Liberians mine iron ore, gold, and other minerals.

What is school like in Liberia?

Children in Liberia must finish 12 years of school. They spend six years in elementary school and six years in secondary school.

During Liberia's civil war, few children went to school. Some of them were forced to join the army. Others were afraid to leave their houses. Many schools were damaged by the fighting.

In Liberia, some students wear uniforms to school. ➤

Some Liberian students have classes in rooms made from palm leaves, dried grass, and wood.

Today, the government wants all children to have an education. Leaders passed a new law to provide free elementary education. People from other countries help Liberian schools. They train teachers and find buildings to hold classes.

What are Liberia's favorite sports and games?

Soccer is one of Liberia's most popular sports. Children enjoy playing and watching soccer with friends. Liberia's national soccer team is called the Lone Star. It is named for the star on Liberia's flag. The team competes in the World Cup and other events.

Fact!

In 1995, Liberian soccer star George Weah was named World Player of the Year by the Fédération Internationale de Football Association. He is the only African player ever to win this award.

Children in Liberia enjoy playing soccer with friends.

Liberians enjoy playing a board game called *kpo*. Different types of this ancient game are played all over Africa. *Kpo* players try to collect the most seeds or small stones from the game board.

What are the traditional art forms in Liberia?

Wood carving and weaving are Liberian art forms. Artists carve wooden masks and musical instruments. Weavers make screens and mats from **bamboo**. They create designs using different colored strips.

Cloth dying is another popular art form. Liberians dye stripes and patterns onto shirts, dresses, and other clothing.

A Liberian man weaves strips of bamboo into a large mat. ▶

A Liberian man dries dyed clothing on a roof in Monrovia.

Liberians also enjoy telling stories. People in Liberia have shared the same tales for hundreds of years. Many of them were never written down. Today, older people teach younger people their stories.

What major holidays do Liberians celebrate?

Liberians celebrate Independence Day on July 26. On this day in 1847, Liberians signed their Declaration of Independence from the United States.

Liberians celebrate many other national holidays. On the first Thursday in November, families gather for Thanksgiving Day. On November 29, Liberians celebrate President William Tubman's birthday. Tubman was Liberia's president for 27 years. He served from 1944 to 1971.

What other holidays do people in Liberia celebrate?

Armed Forces Day
Literacy Day
National Redemption Day
Pioneers' Day

Some Liberians wear traditional headdresses during celebrations.

Liberians celebrate holidays with family and friends. They often go to soccer games. They also eat meals together, play music, and have dances.

What are the traditional foods of Liberia?

Rice and vegetables are common at any Liberian meal. Families often eat peppers, sweet potatoes, yams, and green bananas. They also enjoy cassava. Liberians mash this root vegetable to make a dish called *dumboy*. They also add cassava to soups.

Fact!

Since the civil war, many Liberians do not have enough to eat. Groups from around the world are trying to help. They send rice, canned fish, biscuits, nuts, and other supplies to needy families.

A Liberian child cooks stew on a fire.

Liberians use fish and meat in many dishes. They eat chicken, beef, and fish in many different stews. Most recipes include spinach leaves, palm oil, and hot peppers. Some cooks add okra and pumpkin seeds.

What is family life like in Liberia?

During the civil war, family life changed for many Liberians. Thousands of families lost their homes. Many children lost their parents. Today, families often live in camps for people without houses. Groups from other countries provide homes for children without parents.

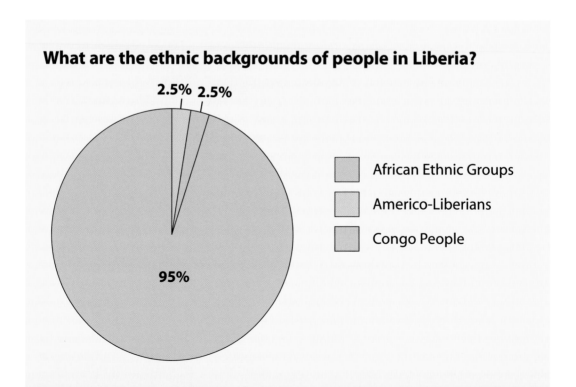

What are the ethnic backgrounds of people in Liberia?

2.5% 2.5%

95%

- African Ethnic Groups
- Americo-Liberians
- Congo People

Since the civil war, many Liberian families live at camps for people without houses.

In Liberia, some children learn traditional **customs** from ethnic social groups. These groups include the Sande and the Poro. The Sande teach girls the skills to become young women. The Poro teach boys the skills to become young men.

Liberia Fast Facts

Official name:

Republic of Liberia

Population:

3,390,635 people

Land area:

*37,189 square miles
(96,320 square kilometers)*

Capital city:

Monrovia

**Average annual
precipitation:**

206 inches (523 centimeters)

Languages:

English and 20 African languages

**Average January
temperature:**

*79 degrees Fahrenheit
(26 degrees Celsius)*

Natural resources:

gold, iron ore, rubber, timber

**Average July
temperature:**

*76 degrees Fahrenheit
(24 degrees Celsius)*

Religions:

African beliefs	*40%*
Christian	*40%*
Islamic	*20%*

Money and Flag

Money:

Liberia's money is the Liberian dollar. One Liberian dollar equals
100 Liberian cents. In 2004, 1 U.S. dollar equaled 99 Liberian cents.
One Canadian dollar equaled 75 Liberian cents.

Flag:

Liberia's flag is called the Lone Star. It is designed after the U.S. flag.
Eleven red and white stripes stand for the 11 signers of Liberia's Declaration
of Independence. A blue square in the upper-left corner stands for Africa.
The star stands for Liberia as Africa's first republic.

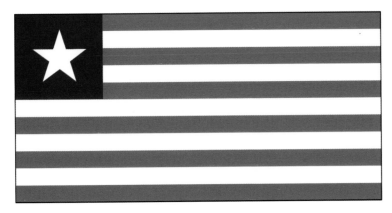

Learn to Speak Kpelle

English is Liberia's official language. But most people speak one of 20 African ethnic group languages. Kpelle is the largest ethnic group in Liberia. Learn to speak some Kpelle words using the chart below.

English	Kpelle	Pronunciation
cat	nj àlè	(NYAH ahl-EE)
crocodile	fà lì	(FAH LEE)
monkey	kwala	(KWAH-la)
squirrel	ló	(LOH)

Glossary

bamboo (bam-BOO)—a tropical plant with a hard, hollow stem

constitution (kon-stuh-TOO-shuhn)—the written system of laws in a country that state the rights of the people and the powers of government

civil war (SIV-il WOR)—war between groups of people in the same country

custom (KUHSS-tuhm)—a tradition in a culture or society

ethnic (ETH-nik)—related to a group of people and their culture

export (EKS-port)—to send and sell goods to other countries

independent (in-di-PEN-duhnt)—free from the control of other people or things

plantation (plan-TAY-shuhn)—a large farm found in warm areas where crops such as coffee, tea, tobacco, and cotton are grown

rebel (REB-uhl)—someone who fights against a government or the people in charge of something

republic (ree-PUHB-lik)—a government headed by a president with officials elected by the people

settlement (SET-uhl-muhnt)—a small village or group of houses

Internet Sites

FactHound offers a safe, fun way to find Internet sites related to this book. All of the sites on FactHound have been researched by our staff.

Here's how:
1. Visit *www.facthound.com*
2. Type in this special code **0736837558** for age-appropriate sites. Or enter a search word related to this book for a more general search.
3. Click on the **Fetch It** button.

FactHound will fetch the best sites for you!

Read More

Miller, Debra A. *Liberia.* Modern Nations of the World. San Diego: Lucent Books, 2004.

Ng, Yumi. *Welcome to Liberia.* Welcome to My Country. Milwaukee: Gareth Stevens, 2004.

Rozario, Paul. *Liberia.* Countries of the World. Milwaukee: Gareth Stevens, 2003.

Weintraub, Aileen. *Discovering Africa's Land, People, and Wildlife.* Continents of the World. Berkeley Heights, N.J.: MyReportLinks.com Books, 2004.

Index